W9-BDV-381

Louisiana Life Series, No. 3

Second Linin'

Jazzmen of Southwest Louisiana, 1900-1950

by
Austin Sonnier, Jr.

Published by The Center for Louisiana Studies
University of Southwestern Louisiana
Lafayette, Louisiana

Cover illustration: Willie Geary "Bunk" Johnson

Library of Congress Catalog Number: 89-81159
ISBN Number: 0-940984-50-4

CONTENTS

Introduction v

Chapter I
Lawrence Duhé, 1887-1960: Jazz Pioneer 1

Chapter II
Willie Geary "Bunk" Johnson 7

Chapter III
Hypolite Charles Interview 18

Chapter IV
Harold Potier—Musician/Sculptor 26

Chapter V
Mercedes Fontenette Potier: Pianist 35

Chapter VI
Jazz Talk: Harold Potier and Morris Dauphine 44

Chapter VII
The Banner Orchestra 54

Chapter VIII
Other Area Bands and Musicians 57

Sources 62

INTRODUCTION

That part of Louisiana which lies west of New Orleans and Baton Rouge has for years been a spawning ground for some of that state's most popular musicians. Originally settled by the French, and the Spanish a bit later, Southwest Louisiana soon became a haven for exiled Acadians and a place of refuge for Haitian sugarcane planters fleeing the army of Toussaint L'Ouverture. These people, Native Americans, and blacks from Africa and the Caribbean lived together in a harmony that produced a unique society responsible for a tradition found nowhere else in the United States, a rural situation that defies association with any other. It is as if an invisible wall had been placed around the area to prevent entry of outside influences and provide sanctuary for the growth of another country within the state.

Of the many types of music that came out of the area, two very distinct forms are currently enjoying worldwide appeal. One is a mixture of European melodic/harmonic structures, African/Caribbean rhythms and vocal lines that are sung in Cajun and Creole patois with peculiar twists in the melody. These sounds, popularly known as Cajun music, were pioneered by black accordionist Amédé Ardoin and white violinist Dennis McGee. They played and recorded together regularly during the 1920s and 1930s. The other form, a younger and extremely popular style, is known as zydeco. While retaining most of the cosmetics of Amédé Ardoin's music, zydeco was taken a step farther by adding blues scales and harmonies and the popular rhythm and blues back beat.

Another form of music which has since the early 1950s fallen from popularity among both musicians and audiences alike is a unique type of rural jazz. This genre, a combination of traditional New Orleans jazz, ragtime, African rhythms, Creole folk material, and the blues was from the beginning of this century a most desirable vehicle for many types of entertainment in Southwest Louisiana. The jazz music of New Orleans filtered through to that part of the state during the early part of this century and immediately influenced local musicians to try their hand at its beauty and charm. This resulted in the birth of a brother to the original New Orleans sounds. So while jazz was prospering in New Orleans it was also alive and moving, albeit at a much slower pace, in Southwest Louisiana. New Orleans had Buddy Bolden; Southwest Louisiana had Evan Thomas. Both places were able to boast of Bunk Johnson.

v

Quite a few of the area's jazzmen travelled to New Orleans when their careers were well along and went on to make names for themselves in jazz history. Others stayed in the city for only a short while, then returned home to the comforts and security of small-town life. And there were others who chose not to move at all. One example is cornetist Hypolite Charles, who was musically active in Parks, Louisiana, around the time Buddy Bolden was at the height of his popularity in New Orleans. When young Charles arrived in the city, at seventeen, he found the music to be similar to that played by the Vitale Band of Loreauville, Louisiana, and the United Brass Band of Parks. He immediately went to work with Manuel Parez's band. Another example is clarinetist Lawrence Duhé who played in New Orleans and Chicago before moving to Lafayette, where, from 1932 to 1945, he played with Evan Thomas' Black Eagles Band, Gus Fontenette's Banner Orchestra, and Frank Brown's Band. Bassist Chester Zardis left New Iberia for New Orleans in 1914 and spent the rest of his life performing there. Those who chose not to leave Southwest Louisiana at all were instrumental in putting together some of the most enduring bands and orchestras in the area.

This work is intended to be an introduction to those men and women, the bands they played in, the places they worked and what their musical lives were all about. There are five major areas of Southwest Louisiana that are covered here: Parks, Lafayette, New Iberia, Crowley and Opelousas. Each contributed to the overall picture of jazz in that region of the state.

LAWRENCE DUHÉ 1887-1960: JAZZ PIONEER

By the early 1900s, New Orleans had become the absolute and undisputed capital of the new music called jazz. Imposing figures like Buddy Bolden, Bunk Johnson and Jelly Roll Morton all roamed the streets and alleys headed for places like Pete Lala's tonk, the Twenty-Five Saloon or Vic Dubois' place on Rampart Street to play their music, down more than a few drinks, and talk shop. The city was alive with all types of music, and the African-French-Spanish traditions that formed a blanket over this heaven of the South provided for a large number of diverse situations where musicians, especially practitioners of the "new" music, could present their talents. During the daytime there were jobs in parades of every sort, advertising dances on the back of horse-drawn wagons, and, of course, the unique New Orleans jazz funerals. Nights brought the musicians into juke-joints, saloons, and dance halls where the music was loud, the women beautiful, and the fights often. The music complemented. It embraced the city and provided a means from which life could draw and experience elation at its fullest.

It was in this atmosphere, around 1914, that clarinetist Lawrence Duhé first noticed his affinity with the music and started seriously to live jazz.

Duhé's musical talent was nurtured by a family of musicians. He began playing the blues at a very early age in La Place, Louisiana, his hometown. His father, Everiste Duhé, worked at the La Place Sugar Refinery as a dryer, and played violin in his own band as well as with other groups in and around town. It was because of his prompting that young Lawrence began to play first the guitar and later the clarinet. He became proficient enough on both instruments to influence his brothers, Gaston, B. L., and Dedana, to take him into their ensemble, The Duhé Brothers' Band. They played the blues, "hot" arrangements of popular songs of the day, and a number of jazz tunes that seeped out of New Orleans with an air of abandon that was reminiscent of the Crescent City. Everything was played by ear. Gaston was the bass player; Blace (B. L.) Duhé, who was to graduate later from Harvard and practice medicine in Beaumont, Texas, played guitar; Dedana, the oldest brother, played trombone and violin; and Lawrence performed on guitar and clarinet. Although their mother did not project a talent for music, two of their sisters did. Both girls played piano and organ in church and at home for the family and friends.

By 1911, in spite of having saddled himself with a job hauling mail for the La Place Post Office, Lawrence was at the height of his involvement with the family band. His love for music, by this time, was beginning to blossom, and soon he started looking to more professional musical situations for aesthetic satisfaction. But not being quite ready to take on New Orleans, he accepted the next best thing, a job in trombonist Ed "Kid" Ory's band.

In Ory's group he was required to play only the clarinet. This led to an attitude which caused him to abandon completely the guitar and to concentrate solely on the wind instrument. As a result, he played clarinet for the rest of his musical career.

In 1913 Ory took the band to New Orleans. Battles of bands and top-notch musicianship were the order of the day, and Kid Ory's band, being one of young men with musically tight arrangements and unending ambition, succeeded in beating Bab Frank's band of seasoned professionals in a fierce cutting contest that was held in Dixie Park. After the victory the band's members decided to stay in New Orleans to seek their fame and fortune in the overcrowded and competitive music underworld. John Joseph's barber shop at Freret and Robinson streets became their headquarters.

For Lawrence Duhé this was a time for learning. He concerned himself solely with the art and trade of music. From Ory and some of the more seasoned veterans of New Orleans music he learned the art and qualities of leadership, a quality born of innate abilities and consciously and systematically digested. From the masters, Lorenzo Tio, Jr., and George Baquet, he studied European concepts of classical clarinet playing. He found himself in an ideal situation.

Duhé's aggressive bearing shortly took him out of the ranks as sideman and into the fore as a leader of his own band. His first venture was at the 101 Ranch, a job that lasted just shy of three months. It was long enough, however, to enkindle the fire that was needed for him to move forward, ever looking for success. Members of this first band were chosen from the city's finest. Personnel included Walter Decou on piano, the great Johnny St. Cyr played guitar, Sidney Desvigne was the cornet player and John Benoit, from Pass Christian, Mississippi, was the drummer. Duhé managed to keep them together and working for about a year in places like Pete Lala's and Tom Anderson's Annex.

In the infant years of this century jazz began to defy geographical restrictions and began to move slowly north, west, and east, spreading itself in a fashion that was no less grander than the times. This advance, especially to Kansas City and Chicago, is well documented. Duhé left New Orleans for Chicago in 1917. Within a short while he and his band were booked into the Deluxe Cafe on Thirty-fifth and State streets. They played there from 8 p.m. until midnight, then rushed off to the Royal Gardens where they performed from 1 a.m. to 4 a. m., seven days a week. This band was one of Duhé's best. It included "Sugar Johnny" Smith on cornet, Roy Palmer on trombone, guitarist Louis Keppard, drummer Fred "Bebe" Hall, Wellman Breaux on bass, and Lil Hardin, whom Duhé later introduced to Louis Armstrong, played piano. The fantastically talented Bill Robinson was a featured dancer in the floor show.

When "Sugar Johnny" Smith died of pneumonia in the winter of 1918, cornet player Mutt Carey was chosen to replace him. Carey accepted the job, but soon found himself in a rather precarious position. Not ever having had the occasion to travel far from the Sun Belt and lacking proper cold weather attire, he was soon compelled to reconsider his decision. He left the band without notice to return to the warm climate of South Louisiana. Once back in New Orleans he influenced Joe Oliver, who was leaving for Chicago to another job, to fill the trumpet chair in the Duhé outfit. "King" Oliver subsequently joined the band when it moved to the Dreamland Ballroom. Things worked out well for a while, but then a bit of trouble arose between Duhé, Joe Oliver, and trombonist Roy Palmer when Oliver insisted that Duhé fire Palmer for sleeping on the bandstand. Duhé, for personal reasons, would not. Differences could not be settled, and in 1919 the trouble suddenly climaxed. The end was as much a surprise to Duhé as was the beginning. When the dust settled, Joe Oliver was the leader of his own orchestra, and Duhé and Palmer were left without a band.

Before this unfortunate occurrence though, Duhé had the honor of leading the first jazz band to play at a World Series game. It was the Cincinnati Red Sox versus the Chicago White Sox series of 1919. Other members of that band were Jimmy Palao on tenor saxophone, George Field on trombone, trumpeter Joe Oliver, Willie Humphrey playing second clarinet, Emmett Scott on banjo, bass player Wellman Breaux (Braud, Brieux), and Minor Hall on drums.

In 1923 Duhé became ill from an ulcer that had been bothering him for some time. It was probably caused in part by the rigors of leading his own band and by the fast-paced lifestyle he adopted after leaving New Orleans.

His doctor advised him to move to Arizona but he headed down south to New Orleans instead.

After a period of restoring himself musically in the city Duhé met Jack Carey who persuaded him to join his excursion circuit which ran from New Orleans to Lafayette. As fate would have it, on Duhé's first trip to Lafayette he was met at the train station by Evan Thomas, the legendary trumpet player from Crowley, Louisiana, and some members of his Black Eagles Band. Thomas, having heard of Duhé's track record, was quick to offer him a job—thirty-five dollars a week plus room and board. Duhé accepted on the spot and was rushed off to Crowley with nothing but his clarinet to play a dance that night. Later, the young lady who managed the boarding house where he was staying helped him get some clothes and other needs. This young lady, Clara, soon became his wife. They eventually moved to Lafayette, settled into a house that was near the hub of black nightlife, and started working on a family.

His association with Evan Thomas lasted about ten years. During that time he also worked with trombone player Gustave Fontenette's Banner Orchestra in New Iberia. "Bunk" Johnson, the famous trumpet player who claimed to have given Louis Armstrong his first lessons in jazz, was living in New Iberia at the time and was developing his highly melodic second-trumpet style as a member of Fontenette's orchestra. Together they travelled throughout Louisiana and Texas. After Evan Thomas was murdered at a dance hall in Rayne, Louisiana, in 1932, Bunk went his way, and Duhé chose to go on the road with the popular Rabbits Foot Minstrels and toured most of the South.

Being away from his wife for long periods of time was not the ideal situation for Duhé, and after a few months he left the Rabbits Foot Minstrels job to join Frank Brown's band back home in Lafayette. Except for a week with Pinchback Touro's Lincoln Band at a fair in Morgan City, Louisiana, in the mid 1930s, Duhé played regularly with Brown until 1945 at a Lafayette restaurant.

That year marked the end of his career as a professional musician. For some reason he no longer considered music to be a part of his life. He constantly refused jobs, including an offer from Kid Ory to join him in California. The desire to perform was no longer there. He lived quitely with his memories, surrounded by pictures of musicians he had played with, his old clarinet and soprano saxophone, records, and other paraphernalia collected during his years in the music business.

Duhé had written three songs in the late 1920s that were recorded on the Cinerama Song Company label of Beverly Hills, California. Copies of "The Lafayette Stomp," "The Evangeline Blues," and "I Like to Take My Girl to the Bathing Beach" are now hard to find. He made no other recordings, a fate common to many old-timers.

Duhé died quitely in his Lafayette home at age seventy-three. He did not get the traditional New Orleans jazz funeral, but most of the musicians with whom he was at one time associated attended funeral services. After services his body was taken to Reserve, Louisiana, for burial.

Thus was the end of another giant of that music called jazz. He is still remembered by some, forgotten by many. A valuable asset to the birth and growth of early Black Classical Music.

Lawrence Duhé at home in Lafayette, Louisiana in 1956.

I LIKE TO TAKE MY GIRL TO THE BATHING BEACH

by
Lawrence Duhé

I like to take my girl
To the bathing beach.
Just to realize the sport
It can't be beat.

You meet other girls and boyfriends
Who join us with a smile.
Boat rowing, fish catching,
A little drinking now and then.

Remember the old umbrella
Is always at hand,
To secure a comfort seat
Right on the sand.

Why worry when you're in reach
To be with your own little peach.
I like to take my girl
To the bathing beach.

II

WILLIE GEARY "BUNK" JOHNSON

According to his death certificate "Bunk" Johnson was born in New Orleans on December 27, 1880, to Thresa Jefferson and William Johnson. He became interested in music early and began taking lessons at seven years old from his school's music teacher, Wallace Cutchey. A year later he started on cornet and progressed rapidly, playing both by music and by ear. For reasons relating mostly to economics, Bunk had to drop out of school when he was fifteen years old. That year, 1895, he got his first job as a professional musician, playing in a reading orchestra that was led by barber Adam Olivier. His time within the confines of the Olivier orchestra was short, and after a year he moved to Charles "Buddy" Bolden's blues band. It is well known that Buddy Bolden's band was the first New Orleans unit to play blues, ragtime, and jazz material and is considered a parent of New Orleans traditional jazz. Bunk played with this band, on and off, for four years.

In early 1900 Bunk played at Frankie Spano's club with "Jelly Roll" Morton on piano and Jimmy Parker on drums. He also played with Jelly Roll at Hattie Rogers' sporting house. During this period he worked with an assortment of orchestras and brass bands in and around New Orleans. He was a regular at Tom Anderson's famed dance hall and also played with pianist-vocalist Mamie Desdunes for a while. But the lure of vaudeville was soon to attract Bunk to the road, and for the next few years he spent his musical energies in minstrel companies and with the P. G. Loral Circus and the Hagenbeck-Wallace Circus, travelling across the United States and England.

By 1910 Bunk was back in New Orleans, playing with Billy Marrero's Superior Orchestra. Members included Buddy Johnson on trombone, "Big Eye" Louis Nelson on clarinet, Walter Brundy on drums, Richard Payne on guitar, and Peter Bocage on violin. Bunk stayed with the Superior Orchestra until 1911 when he joined Frankie Dusen's Eagle Band, an outgrowth of the old Buddy Bolden Band. During this time, between 1910 and 1914, Bunk perfected his form as a jazz musician. He worked with all of the legends: Jelly Roll Morton, Joe "King" Oliver, John Robichaux, Tony Jackson. Bunk influenced Sidney Bechet to join the Eagle Band. Headquarters for the band was a drinking establishment on South Rampart and Perdido streets,

Bunk Johnson in 1942.

The Superior Orchestra between 1907 and 1910. The Superior was one of the first Creole orchestras to play hot music and blues at the turn of the century. Bassist Billy Marrero was the leader. Upon Bunk's return to New Orleans, after about five years on the road with different minstrel and circus bands, he joined up with the Superior. Working regularly with this band, Frankie Dusen's Eagle Band, and John Robichaux's orchestra, Bunk helped establish the New Orleans jazz music tradition. Back row: Buddy Johnson, Bunk Johnson, "Big Eye" Louis Nelson, Billy Marrero. Front row: Walter Brundy, Peter Bocage, Richard Payne.

called the Eagle Saloon. The band took its name from the saloon. Band members included Bunk on cornet, Dusen on trombone, Sidney Bechet on clarinet, Brock Mumford on guitar, Dandy Lewis on bass, and Henry Zeno on drums. Their music was "hot," and they soon became the most popular uptown band at the time.

After a while, Bunk left Dusen to play in the cabarets of the red light district (Storyville). Occasionally, he worked with John Robichaux's orchestra, which for years was "the" band in New Orleans and in constant demand. They were booked in the most desirable spots in the city, including the Grunewald and Antoine's. Each Monday night Robichaux worked at the Masonic Hall in uptown New Orleans where he played all styles of music, from quadrilles to rags. Bunk became well known for his mellow tone, refined melodic taste, and fluid execution. This was, by far, his best musical period. Tours with trombonist Jack Carey took Bunk through most of the small towns in Southwest Louisiana. At a dance in New Iberia he played "Casey Jones" and excited the audience to the extent that they wanted to carry him around the hall on their shoulders. During this period, Bunk played with at least fourteen bands, including some of New Orleans' best.

In 1914, Bunk left New Orleans permanently. He toured with the Georgia Smart Set, a vaudeville-minstrel show, and with the Veron Brothers Circus throughout most of the South and Southwest. He also worked in Chicago and New York City. He taught school in Mandeville, Louisiana, for a year, then moved to Bogalusa where he joined the Fritz Family Orchestra at the Colonial Hotel. In 1916 he was in the Royal Orchestra in Lake Charles, and a year later, with Walter Brundy in Baton Rouge. He also worked with trumpeter Evan Thomas' Black Eagles Band in Crowley, Louisiana, and with Gustave Fontenette's Banner Orchestra in New Iberia. By 1920, Bunk had chosen New Iberia as his permanent place of residence.

New Iberia, a small town to the west of New Orleans located in a part of the state known as Acadiana, was, at that time, a hotbed of jazz musicians. The area cradled a musical awareness similar to that which existed in New Orleans, albeit on a much smaller scale. There were a few jobs available for parades, but most work existed in nightclubs and at sponsored dances. Bunk found a new life for himself there, and embarked on what was to become another eventful, though more subdued, career in music. The bulk of his activity was divided between the Banner band and the Black Eagles Band. By this time Bunk was in his late thirties and a well-seasoned, widely travelled musician.

For the next twenty years Bunk worked in and around New Iberia mostly. His forays out of town included work with the house band at the American Theater in Houston, Texas, which featured such singers as the popular blues shouter Ma Rainey. He did more vaudeville work and even got an offer to join Joe "King" Oliver in Chicago, but turned it down. In 1931 he travelled to Kansas City where he worked the Yellow Front Cafe with pianist Sammy Price, drummer "Baby" Lovett, and vocalist Julia Lee. This was of brief duration, and he was soon back in New Iberia with the Black Eagles Band and Banner band.

The Banner Orchestra was a fairly large ensemble. It consisted of two trumpets, trombone, three reeds, piano, bass, banjo, and drums. It was a reading orchestra that concentrated mostly on jazz treatment of the popular tunes of the time. Gus Fontenette, leader of the orchestra, was a fine musician who insisted on perfection and got it by hiring the best musicians in the area and from as far away as New Orleans. When work for the Black Eagles was slow, Evan Thomas played in the Banner band to make ends meet. He played first trumpet, and Bunk played second. It was in this context that the second-trumpet style incorporated by Bunk was exploited to its fullest. His innate ability at melodic invention combined with a crisp tone and faultless phrasing was the perfect lace to Evan's lead trumpet, which was forceful and could be very loud. Thomas was rooted deeply in the Joe "King" Oliver approach to the trumpet. Older musicians that remember Bunk as a young musician in New Orleans all agree that his trumpet playing was light and melodic even then. He did not hold his notes very long, giving the impression of constantly playing staccato, and his use of chords, particularly in downward phrases, revealed a musical knowledge that was a bit more involved than that of his contemporaries.

During his years in New Iberia, Bunk started having trouble with his teeth. He had to have some of the front ones taken out. This to a trumpet player is quite a handicap as the front teeth act as a foundation of sorts to accept mouthpiece pressure needed to play high notes. But since Bunk used very little pressure in his playing, the problem presented was a bit less than if he had practiced full pressure. According to Banner band members Bunk would take a piece of string and reinforced his embouchure by tying it to his existing teeth to form a bridge that would fill the gap. How well this worked for him is obvious in the urgent requests he later made for a set of false teeth. At any rate, he played light and flowery phrases, and his knowledge of music enabled him to function closer to a clarinetist's point of view. Unlike other trumpeters of traditional New Orleans music Bunk chose to explore the trumpet's alter ego as a delicate instrument capable of producing melodically interesting lines and colors.

He also played the tenor saxophone and tuba on occasion. The latter almost replacing the trumpet for a while. The tenor saxophone, with its low and soulful range, has to this day been the trumpet's most compatible partner. The marriage of the two has lasted with the jazz tradition. Bunk was at home on this instrument simply because of its understatement and power as a melodic voice. He used the instrument in small group settings, incorporating with the lead instrument parallel harmonic lines as well as the customary contrapuntal figures. The embouchure used to play the tenor saxophone was less demanding than that of the trumpet because it was so relaxed. And the dark, legato phrases, which dominated the instrument's role during that time, could be produced easily by Bunk.

Things went along as well as can be expected. About ninety percent of Bunk's support came solely from his music. In addition to the Banner band and Black Eagles he worked with the Washington Band in Cade, Louisiana, the Vitale Band of Loreauville, and Yelpin' Hounds of Crowley on occasion. He also led his own band for special dance jobs, one of them being at the famed Good Hope Hall in Lafayette. During the day he gave private music and trumpet lessons at his home on Franklin [now Malain] Street, but a tragic event was looming that would soon affect him deeply.

In 1932, while playing a dance in Rayne, Louisiana, with the Black Eagles Band, Bunk and New Orleans clarinetist George Lewis witnessed the

The Black Eagle Band in Crowley, Louisiana, around 1924. Left to right: Abraham Martin, Minor Decou, Lawrence Duhe, Robert Goby, Walter Thomas, Joe Avery Evan Thomas. Buck Johnson was playing in Evan Thomas' band the night Thomas was murdered.

murder of Evan Thomas. It was a tragedy that would haunt Bunk for the rest of his life. As the story goes, while the band was playing, a customer approached the bandstand and requested them to play "I'll Be Glad When You're Dead You Rascal You". Band members knew the customer as John Gilbey, a fellow of dark character who had just recently been released from prison. Evan was reputed to have had a not-too-discreet love affair with Gilbey's wife while he was incarcerated. Gilbey somehow got wind of it, and vowed to get even. In the middle of the tune he jumped on the bandstand, pulled a large knife and proceeded to viciously cut and stab Evan. After Evan ran from the nightclub mortally wounded, his attacker went completely berserk and wrecked the bandstand, smashing most of the instruments, including Bunk's trumpet. That incident resulted in a drastic decrease in Bunk's performing activity. Without a horn he could not work, and his teeth were still a problem. He would borrow fellow Banner band member Harold Potier's trumpet to make an occasional gig but most of the time he was musically inactive.

For the next few years Bunk's performing activity could best be described as hit-and-run. He had begun drinking quite heavily, and his ambition to play lessened with the declining nightclub scene. For four years he worked with the New Iberia Public School System as a music teacher under the federally sponsored WPA program. He was instrumental in teaching young and aspiring musicians the basics for a successful career in the field. His work included private lessons, directing ensembles, and teaching music theory. When the WPA laid him off he worked as a truck driver or laborer for various business places in New Iberia, including KONRICO, one of the largest rice distributors in the state. Like many people of this era, he accepted any type work that was available in order to make ends meet.

In 1937 a group of jazz critics and enthusiasts that included Frederic Ramsey, Jr., Charles E. Smith, Stephen W. Smith, and William Russell were planning the first book to be published in America on jazz. While gathering material William Russell learned of Bunk from Louis Armstrong and pianist-publisher, Clarence Williams. Armstrong had met Bunk while playing at a school in New Iberia that frequently featured popular musicians from New Orleans and elsewhere. He could not attest to Bunk's present musical abilities but remembered him as one of the first men to play jazz in New Orleans. The many stories he told of Bunk's exploits and his influence on other musicians caused the writing team to seek out the musician. William Russell wrote a letter to Bunk in care of the New Iberia postmaster because he didn't have an address. Fortunately, the postmaster knew of

Bunk Johnson in 1942.

Bunk Johnson, "the old colored trumpet player from New Orleans," and directed Russell's letter to him. There followed an extensive and fruitful correspondence. Although Bunk provided Russell with a wealth of information relating to New Orleans Jazz and its practitioners, his primary objective was to get the help he needed to start playing the trumpet again. He made his intentions clear by informing Russell that if he could get a set of false teeth and a horn he was sure of still having the technique to play the music he was writing him about. After all, he did have first-hand knowledge of Buddy Bolden, having played with him at the turn of the century, and he was one of the pioneers of the early music. By the winter of 1942 mainly through the efforts of Bill Russell, Bunk had his new teeth. They were made for him in New Orleans by Dr. Leonard Bechet, who was also a musician and the brother of soprano saxist Sidney Bechet. He also received a trumpet that was supposed to have been personally selected by Louis Armstrong. In the spring of that same year, after quite a bit of "woodshedding," Bunk felt that he was ready to play in public again. He sent Russell a home recording he had made of Scott Joplin's "Maple Leaf Rag" along with a letter describing his rekindled enthusiasm. No one, however, was impressed with Bunk's performance on the recording. It was

Bunk with Lawrence Marrero on banjo and George Lewis on clarinet.

Bunk Johnson with the Sidney Bechet Quintet in Boston, Mass. in 1945. From left, Fred Moore, Pops Foster, Bunk, Sidney Bechet and Hank Duncan.

The Bunk Johnson Band in New York in 1945. After his discovery in New Iberia by William Russell, Bunk was associated, on frequent occasions, with this group of musicians in performance and recording dates. Back row: Jim Robinson, trombone; Bunk Johnson; Alcide "Slow Drag" Pavageau, bass; Lawrence Marrero, banjo. Front row: Warren "Baby" Dodds, drums; Alton Purnell, piano; George Lewis, clarinet.

not until David Stuart, then proprietor of the Jazz Man Record Shop in Los Angeles, heard the tape that things started to happen. He contacted Bill Colburn and disc jockey Hal McIntyre in San Francisco, to ask them to accompany him to New Iberia to see Bunk and make arrangements to record him. After getting enthusiastic responses from Colburn and McIntyre, Stuart called Bill Russell in Pittsburgh and Eugene Williams in New York. Both agreed to meet him in New Iberia.

By the first week of June, the team had arrived in New Iberia, listened to Bunk's playing, and arranged a recording date at Grunewald's Music Store in New Orleans. On June 11 Bunk recorded his first material with George Lewis on clarinet, Jim Robinson on trombone, Walter Decou on piano, Lawrence Marrero on banjo, Austin Young on bass, and Ernest Rogers on drums. The session was remarkably successful. Thus the rebirth of Bunk's life as a professional musician. He was once again doing the thing he loved best. At the same time he remained the most knowledgeable source of information about a music that had been neglected for nearly twenty years.

From 1942 to 1947 Bunk was one of the most important figures on the jazz scene. He was constantly in demand for concerts and recording sessions. Those were five busy, music-filled years for the old gentleman of jazz as he travelled to San Francisco, New York, Chicago, Boston and Minneapolis, playing with Louis Armstrong, Sidney Bechet, and a host of old friends from New Orleans.

After doing a recording session in New York City in December of 1947, Bunk returned home to New Iberia. A few months later, in 1948, he suffered his first stroke. It left him weak and beaten, and a year later he had another one and died.

Of all the jazzmen that plied their trade in Southwest Louisiana, Bunk was by far the most popular. His contributions to the early jazz music of New Orleans are well documented and his involvement with the New Iberia scene has left certain trademarks in the local music that indicate the influence of his unique musicianship.

III

HYPOLITE CHARLES INTERVIEW

Cornet player Hypolite Charles was born in Parks, Louisiana, on April 18, 1891. The son of a school teacher, he was encouraged in his interest in music by his father, Auguste, and upon organizing his own band prior to going to New Orleans his father joined him as a member. The other musicians in the band were Theophile Thibodeaux on trumpet; Hypolite Potier, cornet; Simon Thibodeaux, trombone; and Gabriel Ledet on bass.

He also played with the Vitale Band in Loreauville, Louisiana, with Jules Day on trumpet; Tom Vitale, second trumpet; Louis Vitale on trombone; and Pierre Vitale on bass. Auguste Charles often joined them on baritone horn. In 1908 Hypolite moved to New Orleans to study music with Eugene Moret, the brother of George Moret, leader of the Excelsior Brass Band. Within a year he was working with Manuel Parez at a dance hall on Dauphine and Elysian Fields. In 1911 he joined the Silver Leaf Orchestra which was led by violinist Albert Batiste. Sam Dutrey played clarinet; his brother, Honore, was on trombone; Phillip Nickerson played guitar; Jimmy Johnson, who had been with Buddy Bolden, played bass; Willie Carter was on drums. The band played mostly for debutante balls and private parties along St. Charles Avenue. Hypolite also began playing parades with the Excelsior Brass Band. While playing for funerals and parades the band would march all over town on streets that were rocky and full of potholes. Once, in the French Quarter, he stumbled over a large rock and cut his lip badly. After that he would not play in the streets with bands that read music. He subsequently joined "Papa" Celestin's Tuxedo Brass Band and remained with it for a number of years.

He joined the Maple Leaf Orchestra in 1919 and opened with them at the Washington Youree Hotel in Shreveport, Louisiana, in July of that year. They came back to New Orleans in the fall, and a few months later Charles organized his own orchestra and started working at the Moulin Rouge. His group composed of Sonny Henry, trombone; Joe Welch, drums; Sam Dutrey, clarinet; Emile Bigard, violin; and Camille Todd, piano. He had studied with Camille Todd in 1909.

When Armand J. Piron went on his second trip to New York, Charles' orchestra replaced him at Tranchina's with only one change in personnel, Robert Hall replaced Dutrey on clarinet.

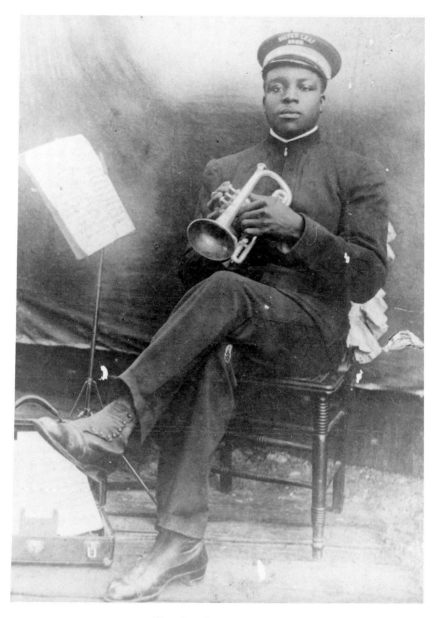

Hypolite Charles in 1911.

Charles retired from playing music in 1925 when, after performing for a Sunday afternoon tea dance, he suffered a ruptured spleen. He was confined to his bed for a year. After getting well he started selling life insurance in New Orleans, and continued to do so until 1940, when he turned his accounts over to Peter Bocage and returned to Parks to take over his father's grocery store.

The following interview took place during the summer of 1975 at Mr. Charles' home in Parks, Louisiana.

AUSTIN SONNIER - When did you play your first funeral job?

HYPOLITE CHARLES - I started playing for funerals when I began playing with Sonny ["Papa"] Celestin's Tuxedo Band . . . Oscar Celestin. We used to call him "The Dog" because of the way he looked in the face. Kind of like a bulldog . . . real mean looking but one of the finest persons I know. It was a pleasure working with him. He was a real gentleman and he didn't go for all that foolishness like a lot of the other musicians did. Music was his business and he took pride in doing it that way. He was responsible. Know what I mean?

There was a lot of musicians, good ones too, that lived that bad life. All they did was stand on the streets and drink and had a lot to do with these women that would hang around the nightclubs. They had a lot of fun. They had a lot of fun, but they didn't live long. All that foolishness is not healthy for you. Well, Mr. Celestin didn't go for all that. He was a respectable person.

Now we played quite a few parades for different lodges and social clubs, but the funeral processions were really something. That was an all-day affair sometimes. First, the band had to meet where the body was . . . at the dead person's house where all the family and friends would be. Then, when the time came, they would take the body out of the house and would all march to the church. No music, just the procession. Well, at the church is where it would all start. Sometimes there would be five or six preachers, and they all had to say something about the dead person. Man, that would take forever. While all of this was going on we would sit outside the church and wait. Some of the fellows who liked to take a little drink would walk over to a barroom and buy beer or something and wait there.

Now after all the ceremonies were over . . . that would sometimes take more than two hours . . . they would take the body out of the church and we would all get together to start the march to the cemetery. Then the work began. You had to walk down these streets that had big holes and rocks all over the place. They didn't have no pavement like today mister. And it was really hard to read from the little hymn book and watch where you were walking. I got hurt that way one time. Fell down and hurt myself real bad.

And those graveyards, some of them was a disgrace. Old, broken-down tombs . . . trash. In fact, there was one that I remember was so bad the city or somebody went in there and cleaned everything out. Tore all the old tombs down and got rid of all the junk. They built a shopping center on that spot.

A. S. - Do you remember the name of that cemetery?

H. C. - No. I can't recall the name right now. But it was bad in those days. People just didn't have the money. I always had a job besides playing music. You had to do that to make ends meet. I worked for the largest bank in New Orleans, and I also sold insurance. I gave Peter Bocage my job when I quit the insurance business to return to Parks.

Well, on the way to the graveyard we would always play slow pieces . . . hymns, to keep the funeral procession moving at a slow pace. People would hear the music and would come on the outside and stand on the street and watch. Some of them would join in the walk to the graveyard. They didn't have to know who was dead. That's the way it was back then.

Once in the graveyard, we would stand back and wait again. There was a bit more to be said over the body then it would be pushed into the tomb. When it was all over . . . ashes to ashes, dust to dust . . . we would assemble again and the person who hired us would give the word for us to lead them out of the graveyard. The drummer would play a roll and the lead trumpet player would start off with "Didn't He Ramble." Then we would move out at a fast pace. Once we got out of the graveyard the hearse would go its way and the family would go their way or sometimes they would follow us for a few blocks.

We only played for a few blocks outside of the graveyard because things usually got real bad with all the people by then. It was a disgrace the way some of them acted. The police would always have to be there to try and keep trouble down.

One thing you should know . . . the Tuxedo Band was the first one to play "When the Saints Go Marching In" at a funeral. All the bands would play "Didn't He Ramble" and one day Oscar Celestin said that he wanted to play something different. The two of us looked through the music book and decided to try "When the Saints Go Marching In". It really went over big. Most of the other bands started playing it after that.

A. S. - Did the band members go to the family's house after the funeral?

H. C. - Oh yes. Sometimes. If the person who died was a good friend or one of the fellows in the band family, they would invite you to go over to eat and drink something. That was done in respect to the dead. (A tradition of African origin that embraces rejoicing at death.) That was like a big party but with no music.

At the wake, before the funeral, everybody would pay their last respect by staying with the body all day and all night . . . praying a lot. It would be a sad time. Then, after the funeral service and the burial was over everybody would meet at the house. All the neighbors and family would cook and bring a pot of something to the house. There would be any kind of food you could name and all the beer and whiskey you could drink. Just the family and close friends would be there. The musicians always tried to go because it meant a free meal.

A. S. - Let's go back to Parks for a while. Did you ever play for parades or funerals there?

H. C. - No. We never had music like that at funerals in Parks . . . not even in New Iberia. As far as I know, that was something that went on only in New Orleans. I don't know how it started, but I do know that they were doing it when I first went there in 1908.

We played for church fairs and outings in Parks. There were some real good musicians there too . . . the Thibodeaux brothers, Hypolite Potier, Beauragard Adam from Cade used to play around here a lot, my father, Auguste Charles . . . all good musicians. Peter Carey used to come all the way from Lafayette to give music lessons and play.

There was a man in Parks called Lemon Ledet. I don't remember exactly what day it was, but he used to give a parade and outing once a year on Lemon Ledet Day. That was his day. All the local musicians would get together and form a big marching band and parade all over town before going to the picnic ground. Parade on both sides of the bayou. We would just play marches. At the outing we would take turns playing music for people to dance to all day long.

Hypolite and his wife, Rose at home in Parks, Louisiana in 1979.

A. S. - The story is that you became so good at playing the cornet you became leader of your own band at a very early age. Was it hard for you to deal with the older and more experienced musicians?

H. C. - No problem at all. Most of us were related one way or the other. It was like one big family. In fact, they were all for me going to New Orleans and getting in the big-time music business there. I was special to them and they were all my teachers and wished me well.

A. S. - Did you ever meet or hear Buddy Bolden?

H. C. - I never did meet him, but Bolden was very popular in New Orleans. He played a lot of blues and ragtime pieces. I played mostly in orchestras that played classical and dance music. Of course we did play blues and ragtime pieces too. My wife, Rose, had an uncle by the name of Fritz who played guitar in Buddy Bolden's band. She can remember when they would practice at his house, but she was just a little girl and didn't know any of the fellows.

A. S. - What about Bunk Johnson. Did you know him in New Orleans?

H. C. - Bunk was all over the place. Real popular. He was a little skinny fellow . . . just like a bird. His cornet style was different from the rest of us because he would play short phrases, and his notes were all short. Stacatto. He wouldn't hold them for their full value. His style was all his own.

When I went to New Orleans in 1908 I started taking music lessons with Eugene Moret who was the brother of George Moret. George was one of the best cornet players in New Orleans. He was also the leader of his own band—the Excelsior. He was a trained musician. Could read anything you put in front of him . . . and could play that jazz too.

Well, that was a good start for me. From my association with the Morets I soon got to know all of the best musicians in the city. Fellows that didn't go for too much foolishness. Know what I mean? . . . Oak and Vic Gaspard, Armand Piron, Camella Todd, Alphonse Picou, Arnold Metoyer, Sam Dutrey . . . all great musicians. I was lucky to even be able to keep up with them. That was pretty fast company.

Camella Todd was a concert pianist and a music teacher. She also played with the Maple Leaf Orchestra for a while. She was known and respected

The Silver Leaf Orchestra in New Orleans in 1911. Left to right: Willie Carter, Hypolite Charles, Sam Dutrey, Sr., Albert Batiste, Phillip Nickerson, and Jimmy Johnson. Missing from the picture is trombone player Honoré Dutrey.

throughout the city. I also studied with her, and we became very good friends.

After a while I started playing here and there with different people, and in 1911 I was offered a job playing with the Silver Leaf Orchestra. That was my first big job. I was twenty years old and learned a lot from those older fellows. Albert Batiste was the leader.

From there, I would say in 1919, I went with the Maple Leaf Orchestra. That was another one of the city's great bands.

A. S. - It seems that most of your time as a musician was spent playing in reading bands. Did you get a chance to improvise much?

II. C. - Yes. We improvised, but not much. Sometimes we would play a blues number or a dance piece that had sections to solo. . . . Hot numbers. In the Tuxedo Band though, most of the tunes were played by ear and you could solo as much as you liked. That was the kind of band those "hot" players liked to be in.

I played with the Excelsior and the Tuxedo. By doing that I got a taste of both styles. You had to read to make it though. That was one of the things I learned when I first moved to New Orleans. Musicians that could read real well got the high-class jobs.

IV

HAROLD POTIER - MUSICIAN/SCULPTOR

Harold Potier was born in Parks, Louisiana, in 1911. His childhood, as far as he remembers, was one filled with music and colorful musicians. His father, Hypolite Potier, was a cornet player with the Hypolite Charles Marching Band of Parks in 1909 and an original member of the Banner Orchestra of New Iberia. He was nicknamed the "Ironman" because of his powerful playing style and endurance. The tag, according to Harold, was given to him during the years he played with marching bands. It seems he was the only man strong enough to march and play all day without getting tired.

When Harold reached the age of twelve he started to think seriously about becoming a professional musician. His father, delighted by the thought of having a young musician in the family, bought him a trumpet and enrolled him in the Oger School of Music in Crowley. There, under the tutelage of one of Louisiana's European trained classical musicians, he studied trumpet, clarinet, saxophone and theory. Professor Oger, a graduate of the Mozart Conservatory of Music in Paris, was a trumpet player of high regard. He had toured throughout Europe and North Africa in the early 1900s with the Paris Symphony, one of the largest orchestras of that time. His knowledge of the instrument was total, and Harold absorbed all that was offered him. In fact, young Potier was such a good student he was soon invited to live with Professor Oger while he continued his studies. This proved to be a very rewarding period in Harold's life. This close master/apprentice relationship caused him to blossom into a trumpet player of top quality while still in his teens. His early association with older, established musicians on a social level also helped. From their advice he was able to develop the frame of mind much needed to grapple with a career of so precarious a future.

Hypolite's dream of bringing up one of his children to be a trumpet player came true when Harold, at the age of 16, received his "Certificate of Excellence in Trumpet and Saxophone" from the Oger School and was invited to join the Banner band. Gus Fontenette, the band's leader was in need of a saxophone player, and Harold seemed a logical choice. He accepted, but with the trumpet on his mind. Probably because of the influence his father had upon him the trumpet had always been his favorite

Hypolite Potier in 1913

horn. On nights the Banner band was not playing he would freelance on trumpet with other local bands. In fact, most of his time was spent either performing, sitting-in, or practicing regularly on that instrument. As his popularity as a trumpet player grew, he gradually moved away from the saxophone until he was finally able to give it up completely.

The last job that he was offered as a saxophonist was in 1932. Evan Thomas, leader of the Black Eagles Band of Crowley, called him to play with the band at a dance hall in Rayne. For reasons relating to another date he had on trumpet Harold was forced to turn the job down, so Evan got clarinetist George Lewis from New Orleans to work the dance with him.

Evan, aside from being a trumpet player of high voltage, had acquired a reputation as a ladies' man. A reputation that, on the very night of this particular dance, was to cost him dearly. While the band was in the middle of "I'll Be Glad When You're Dead You Rascal You," a man named John Gilbey jumped on the bandstand shouting that Evan had been fooling around with his wife. In a frenzy of rage he fatally stabbed Evan after a short, vicious struggle. Evan stumbled through the crowd and got about a block away from the club before he fell dead. After Evan ran from the building and the other musicians had escaped by way of a window, Gilbey went completely berserk and proceeded to smash most of the instruments on the bandstand. Bunk Johnson, who had been playing second trumpet with Evan that night, lost his horn in the confusion.

When the news of the murder got back to Potier in New Iberia, he looked upon the incident as a sign. He had, after all, turned down the job to play his favorite horn, the trumpet, with another band. By associating the saxophone with the negative he was able to reinforce his feelings for the trumpet and began to perform only on the brasswind from that point on.

When Willie Geary "Bunk" Johnson moved from New Orleans to New Iberia in 1921 he brought with him the germ of an innovative approach to playing the trumpet that he later developed to perfection while playing with the Banner Orchestra and the Black Eagles Band. During his early days in New Orleans he had played second trumpet with Buddy Bolden's band. This position required him to function in almost the same manner as a clarinetist. That is, to play melodic phrases around the lead trumpet. His keen sense of rhythm and melody along with a uniquely understated dynamic level introduced a welcomed element to the sound of traditional jazz. Regrettably, he was not allowed to play that role on the many recordings he made in the 1940s.

Potier listened to Bunk play with Evan Thomas. He listened to the beauty of his lines and the pointillistic dancing he did around the melodies of Evan's lead horn. For months he consumed the music, learned to play what he heard and then discarded all but what felt compatible to his style.

The military also extended a hand in the development of Potier's musical talents. In 1942 he was drafted into the army, and for the next three years he played with the 418th Armed Forces Band overseas. His time was well spent. The army made available to him the opportunity to live and play with many top-notch musicians of diverse musical backgrounds. Holding

Harold Potier during World War II when he was a member of the 418th Armed Forces Band.

Harold Potier in 1980.

Harold Potier at his uncle's funeral in St. Martinville in 1977.

down a trumpet chair with the band, he played places like New Zealand, Australia, India, Iran, Egypt and Italy.

After the service Potier returned home to his wife, pianist Mercedes Fontenette, and his job with her father, Gus Fontenette. The years that followed were good ones. He had grown musically. His marriage to the trumpet had become a more complete union in that the horn was finally an extension of his being. His ideas flowed freely and effortlessly and there were no longer the problems of technique to deal with. It was a time he felt most complete as a musician.

There were no recordings though. The Banner Orchestra was never recorded. The Black Eagles were never recorded. Geography, it seems, played a sizable role in this absence of recording activity. New Orleans, where the bulk of music traffic was centered, was too far away and record producers were content with exploiting the talent there anyway. Nobody took much interest in going off to "discover" anyone after Bunk Johnson.

Potier and some of his works in wood.

Surely economic and social factors also played their part. So, the best years
of Potier and some of Louisiana's finest musicians just went up in sound.

Harold continued to play undaunted. He stayed with the Banner Orchestra
until the early 1950s when Gus Fontenette was forced to disband because of
illness. For the next twenty-five years he worked days as a waiter, nights as
a free-lance musician and during his spare time he carved busts, statues and
other objects from wood.

In an attempt to expand his artistic output he had taken courses in art at a
New Iberia trade school in the mid-1940s. During his studies he tried his
hand at different types of media and discovered wood sculpture best suited for
him as far as economics and the availability of materials were concerned.
Working tools were cheap and cypress was plentiful along the bayous and
swamps around New Iberia. So with the same amount of energy that he
placed in his music, Potier launched himself into the world of sculpture. By
the 1970s some of his work commanded as much as $500.

It has been said that music heals. In Potier's case it also served as a preservative and extender of vitality. His life has been one continuous diet of sounds that has kept him alert, energetic, and always looking to the next encounter with a degree of positiveness not found in others his age.

Potier's concept of trumpet technique and improvisation can best be described as being the sum of his blues roots, classical training, and the influence of trumpeter Bunk Johnson. His attack is crisp, his intonation always dead center and his statements complete and to the point, never allowing room for out-of-context frills of energy. Harmonically, he can superimpose, substitute or extend existing chords to fit his unique melodic ability, thus enabling him to play with the fluid-like grace of a clarinetist. He also employs a wry use of "blue notes," a definite influence of Bunk Johnson, by placing them at points which indicate emphasis on the complete statement rather than just the altered note and its accompanying phrase.

A purist in the truest sense of the word, Potier is by far the musically strongest of the few surviving practitioners of early rural Louisiana jazz. His music is indeed an echo of what that particular style was all about.

Mercedes Potier in 1933.

V

MERCEDES FONTENETTE POTIER: PIANIST

The drive to New Iberia on that early autumn morning was a welcome change from the previous week of indoors inactivity. As the trees came into view, rushed by and slowly faded with a gentle swaying, they calmly opened the new day with fantastic surrealistic colors and earthy scents caused by a combination of warm morning sun and the South Louisiana night air. The few houses that dotted the wayside in pointillistic rhythms were still embraced by the invisible blanket of the nocturnal spirits. Only livestock moved about. Cattle . . . chickens . . . a dog here and there. The long hot summer had finally come to an end and the welcomed gift of cool weather was being promised as teasingly as the carrot hanging from the end of the pole.

It had been a bit more than a year since I first met pianist Mercedes Potier and what continued to impress me most was her vitality and especially the power of her musical being. She had been consumed by the piano at a very early age, and the dedication she showered on the instrument and its music was truly of monumental proportion.

Mercedes is the product of a musical family. Her father, Gustave Fontenette, was the leader of the famous Banner Orchestra of New Iberia, Louisiana, from 1920 to the early 1950s. His aunt, Lila William Dusen, was the piano player for vaudeville star Sweet Papa Snowball and the wife of trombone player Frankie Dusen, who became leader of the Eagle Band when its original leader, Buddy Bolden, was committed to a mental institution. One of Mercedes' sisters, Mary Ella, was a music teacher and part-time piano player with local jazz bands. A younger brother, Gustave Jr., played saxophone with blues recording artist Guitar Slim (Eddie Jones) for many years.

Mercedes is a piano player whose style best projected the approach she and her contemporaries embraced in their expression of the music of this area. She displayed a technique that incorporated elements of blues, ragtime, marches, and some of the early jazz material of New Orleans. Not unlike other pianists of the genre, she was a two-handed player and her music contained poly-rhythms and countermelodies of an intricacy that required a total mastery of the instrument.

Mercedes at the piano with the Banner Band during its last years. Gus Fontenette (trombone), Harold Potier (trumpet), Louis Landry (bass), Beauragard Adam (alto saxophone).

Although her tenure in her father's orchestra lasted some thirty years, she also worked sporadically with other bands of the area. For a while she was with trumpeter Evan Thomas' Black Eagles Band from Crowley, Louisiana, and later she did a short stint with the Yelpin' Hounds Band, also from Crowley.

As the countryside vanished from the rear window of the car the sounds, sights, and smells of an awakening city began to slowly greet me. My sports car instinctively snaked up and down narrow streets, across the Bayou Teche, and on to the old Acadian structure that was once a haven for local jazz musicians. I was a bit early. But then that's no problem in a household where life is measured by the beat of a metronome and not of the clock.

Mercedes was waiting. The many years of playing music in some of the best jazz bands of the area were chiseled in the lines of her face. Although it had been nearly twenty years since she worked steady with a band, she had apparently not lost much of her enthusiasm for playing. She had, in fact, turned to school and the church as outlets for her tremendous musical talent.

As a teacher she was able to to keep up with the theory associated with her craft, and as a church organist she was busy enough to keep her technique in fair shape. It was obvious she had never allowed herself the chance to suffer from a lack of activity.

After settling down with the microphone in hand and tape recorder loaded and buzzing its own kind of avant-electro music the interview began.

AUSTIN SONNIER: Let's start with your early years in New Iberia.

MERCEDES POTIER: Well, I was born here. My father's name was Gustave Fontenette and my mother's name was Jennie. As far back as I can remember, there was music around the house, lots of music. My father was a trombone player and a barber. He was also a bartender at times when dance jobs were hard to get. I don't know how much the family was involved in music before his time, but it sure was a big thing with him.

AUSTIN SONNIER: Did he ever talk about other trombone players or musicians in general who might have influenced him musically?

MERCEDES POTIER: No. Not much. But he had an aunt, Lila William was her name, who was a piano player and was married to a trombone player from New Orleans. He was real popular over there. His name was Frankie Dusen. My father used to talk about him a lot. He was a young man around Frankie Dusen's time.

AUSTIN SONNIER: Did Frankie Dusen ever play around New Iberia?

MERCEDES POTIER: That was before my time. I guess he did though. He married Lila and she was from here. King Oliver used to play here all the time; so did Louis Armstrong. Maybe he came over with one of them.

Back in those times there were plenty musicians around New Iberia, and they could all play that jazz too. There were lots of good orchestras and brass bands that would play for parades and church fairs and things. My father formed the Banner Orchestra around 1920 and he never had trouble getting good musicians to play with him. They would even come from New Orleans.

When I started playing with him Evan Thomas from Crowley was playing first trumpet. Talk about a sound. Everybody had to help him read, but boy could he play that horn. You could hear him for blocks around.

My father used him to advertise the band. When we would play in New Iberia, there was a furniture store uptown that would let Evan sit in the window . . . the show-window . . . and play his horn for the people as they passed by. He did that to let them know where we would be playing that night. There was also a hall in Lafayette where we played on the second floor for dances. True Friends Hall might have been the name of it. . . I don't exactly remember. Well, it had all these windows all around the building, and when it was hot they would raise them all up to let the air in. On the day of the dance Evan would go to the hall a few hours early and sit down and play his trumpet out of a window on every side of the place. By the time the dance would start the hall would be packed with people.

Old Bunk (Willie Johnson) began playing in the Banner Band just before he married Maude. He was playing second trumpet. Now that was a musician for you. Bunk could read anything and would play just as pretty as you can imagine. He drank quite a bit and could be real nasty at times, but he had a right to, he knew what music was all about. Me and him got along real well though.

AUSTIN SONNIER: Why did Bunk play second trumpet?

MERCEDES POTIER: Because he played light, short notes and real sweet sounding melodic phrases. While Evan played the melody real loud Bunk would play little melodies around him like a clarinet player. Also, Bunk would not play high notes on the horn. He stayed around the middle register.

A. S.: He started playing that way when he was with Buddy Bolden.

M. P.: Yes. I guess so. Never heard anybody play like that besides Bunk.

A. S.: What about Harold, your husband?

M. P.: Harold was influenced by Bunk, Evan Thomas, and his father, "Iron Man" (Hypolite Potier). He plays short phrases like Bunk did but he sticks close to the melody. Yes . . . I guess you could say that he plays trumpet something like Bunk did.

A. S.: Tell me more about your father.

M. P.: Did you see his trombone? I don't know where Harold put it.

A. S.: Yes. First time I came over . . . .

M. P.: It's got blisters on it (laughter). He used to use a wooden mute. He played real hard and loud and would choke the horn with the mute until blisters would pop up. Glossey Roy, who was a saxophone player in the orchestra, used to tease him about that all the time.

My father wanted all of us to be musicians. He just about got his wish, too. I play piano and organ. My sister, Mary Ella, was a music teacher and piano player. And my brother, Gus Jr., we call him Bubba, is a saxophone player. He has played with Guitar Slim, Joe Tex, T-Bone Walker, Ray Charles, and a lot more people.

When I was young I took piano lessons from a piano teacher, but it was my father and sister who taught me most of my music. How to read and play with the right fingers and all. I majored in music at Xavier University in New Orleans and became good enough to play in my father's band. They played by music and by ear. So you see, I had to know how to read and to improvise.

A. S.: Did you play in any other bands?

M. P.: Oh yes. I played with the Yelpin' Hounds out of Crowley and with the Black Eagles Band, which was Evan Thomas' group. George Lewis, the clarinet player from New Orleans, and Lawrence Duhé also played in that band. I worked a few dances with other small bands around New Iberia, but it was mostly the Banner Orchestra that I stayed with. I started with them in the 1930s and stayed until around 1951.

The Banner Orchestra lasted a long time . . . more than forty years. The best group was when Bunk was in it though. There was Bunk and Evan on trumpets, my father on trombone, Lawrence Duhé, Glossey Roy, and Tom Edwards on reeds, Robert Stafford on drums, William Burner played piano, Edward Reedom [Edwin Redium?] was on violin and guitar, and banjo, and John Sanders from Jeanerette played the bass. That was some band. When Robert Stafford left the orchestra he formed a jazz band called the Night Hawks and played around town for a while.

New Iberia was a good town for jazz musicians. You could make as much money in one night as most people made working at other jobs in a week. That's why Bunk liked it so much over here. He would teach music

John Sanders in November of 1926. Sanders played bass and drums throughout a musical career that lasted from 1902 to the early 1940's.

in the daytime and play at night. Of course he had a few other jobs (non-musical), but they didn't mean nothing to him. He wouldn't stay on them long.

A. S.: What about when he lost his teeth . . . could he play much then?

M. P.: Bunk didn't loose all of his teeth. Just the ones in the front that he needed most to play on. What he did then was he started playing tuba. He would take some string and wind it across the teeth he had to make a support for the mouthpiece when he would play. That worked out well for Bunk because he was a trumpet player who could play without much lip pressure. The tuba worked out well for him until some people from New York [William Russell and friends] bought him a set of false teeth. They made a lot of records of him in the '40s, and he became famous. New Iberia was always his home though.

A. S.: You're from a considerably long blood-line of musicians; so is Harold. Are your children carrying on the tradition?

M. P.: My two sons, Harold Jr. and John, are both accomplished musicians. John plays keyboards and trumpet and has worked with Joe Tex and Bobby Bland. He's the leader of his own band now. Harold Jr. played drums with Bobby Bland for about sixteen years all around the world. Their children will probably grow up to be musicians also. You never know.

A. S.: What kind of music did the Banner Orchestra play? Was it mostly jazz?

M. P.: No. We played a lot of jazz, but we also played popular songs, the blues, and a waltz now and then. It depended where we were playing.

A. S.: Harold told me about the Catholic schools and how you had to play just fast pieces.

M. P.: Yes. When we played for the nuns we couldn't play the blues or any slow pieces. They didn't want the kids dancing close to each other.
   Dance halls were a different story. We played the blues, foxtrot, charleston, and waltz pieces for the old people. It was a lot of fun to play dance halls and nightclubs.

When Bunk came into the band he brought the *Red Back Book of Rags* with him. They played a lot of tunes from that.

A. S.: What about French songs . . . zydeco . . . la la music. Was there much request for that around New Iberia at that time?

M. P.: I guess so . . . I don't really know . . . In fact I can't think of ever hearing that kind of music around here. You find a lot of that around Opelousas where the mulattos live. Most of the musicians I knew played jazz. I'm not saying that they didn't have zydeco here, I just wasn't interested. Beauragard Adam, Abbot Verdun, "Cuddick" (Theodore Richardson), Walter Spencer . . . they all played jazz.

A. S.: Tell me about the marching bands.

M. P.: There were quite a few brass bands around. The United Brass Band from Parks was the most popular. Harold's father, Hypolite Potier, played cornet with them. The band consisted of two trumpets, a cornet, two trombones, the baritone horn player was Hypolite Charles' father, August Charles, who was also a schoolteacher, and there was a drummer. Once a year a man called Lemon Ledet would put on a big parade in Parks and the United Brass Band would play. That was something to see . . . they would really put on a show.
  Hypolite Charles also had a parade and dance band. The Vitale Band would march, and so would a few other bands that I forget the names of.

A. S.: Did they ever play for funerals?

M. P.: No. I never heard of a band playing for a funeral around here. They did a lot of that in New Orleans though. When Walter Spencer died his school band played for the funeral, but that's a different thing.

A. S.: You mentioned that name before. What instrument did Mr. Spencer play?

M. P.: Walter played french horn, string bass, and cello. He was a member of the Banner Orchestra for a while, but he preferred to teach school and only played now and then. (He) was one of the best known band directors in the area. He would come home all the time and talk about music with Bunk and my father.

A. S.: If you had it to do all over again, would there be any changes?

M. P. YES! (laughter) Not too much with the music though.

VI

JAZZ TALK: HAROLD POTIER AND MORRIS DAUPHINE

Trumpeter Harold Potier was born in Parks, Louisiana, in 1911. His father, Hypolite Potier, gave him his first lessons on the cornet. When he was twelve years old he began his formal studies on trumpet, clarinet and saxophone at the Oger School of Music in Crowley. Professor Joseph Oger was a graduate of the Mozart Conservatory of Music. Before his health failed him, he toured with the Paris Symphony throughout Europe.

Potier joined the Banner Orchestra when he graduated from school and stayed on until he was called into the army during World War II. His army stint was spent playing with the 418th Armed Forces Band, touring throughout Europe and North Africa.

After the war he returned to New Iberia where he played with the Banner Orchestra, the Black Eagles Band, the Yelpin' Hounds, and the Jenkins Band. He also worked for a short time with pianist "Sweet Emma" Barrett.

Morris Dauphine was born in Parks in 1906 and played clarinet and saxophone. He left Parks in 1920 to study at the Howe Institute in New Iberia. While in that town he studied clarinet privately with Jimmy Adam, a noted member of the Banner Orchestra and the Adam Family Band. In 1925 he moved to New Orleans to help his uncle operate a drugstore on South Galvez. The intentions of his parents were for him to attend medical school, but after much deliberation he was allowed to try his hand at music. He took lessons with Lorenzo Tio, Jr. After a while he joined Oscar Celestin's Tuxedo Band and stayed with them for two years.

In 1927 he moved to Baton Rouge after accepting an offer to play with the Deluxe Harmony Players, that city's most popular dance band. They were instrumental in raising money for refugees of the destructive 1927 floods by playing benefit concerts and dances.

In 1930, on the advice of his physician, Dauphine stopped playing music and returned to Parks. There, he operated a nightclub for ten years. During this period he would play occasionally with various local bands, including the Banner Orchestra.

The following conversation took place at saxophonist Morris Dauphine's home in New Iberia in the summer of 1974.

HAROLD POTIER - In the old days people used to say that black musicians weren't educated in music. That's what the whites used to say. Hell, just about all of the musicians I knew read music. You had to read if you wanted to play with a band that had any kind of name. Take Bunk Johnson for instance, he finished school in music. He had a good foundation and knew music from the inside out.

MORRIS DAUPHINE - He could stand up with any band and play. Didn't have to practice or anything like that. You had to know music and your instrument to do that. Know what your instrument could do, and most of all, where to find the notes you wanted.

H. P. And if the music weren't there, he could still play.

M. D. - Yes.

H. P. - You see, you found a lot of musicians that were like that. They could play if they had music or not. There was a lot of jammin' and settin' in back in the old days too. That was a school itself because musicians learned a lot from each other that way.

M. D. - In referring to reading music . . .

H. P. - Lots of people said Evan [Thomas] couldn't read. They were wrong. He could read.

M. D. - Well, I never knew too much about Evan. I heard him play quite often though.

H. P. - I knew.

M. D. - That's because you were out there. You had the occasion to be with him.

H. P. - The reason I said he could read music is because him and Bunk used to get into big arguments about music. Do you know where they would go to settle them? At Professor Oger's house in Crowley, that's where.

M. D. - Now that's what I call a great musician. That was a great musician.

H. P. - I lived with him for eight years. He was just like a father to me. That old man knew just about everything about music and he also had one of the best reading bands around. He looked just like a white man . . . was a mulatto though. He studied music in Europe at the Mozart Conservatory. And he played with the Paris Symphony for a long time. His band played nothing but sweet music.

Bunk, the kind of musician he was to me, was a sweet trumpet player. From below the staff and in the staff, he was one of the sweetest trumpet players I ever heard. He had melody down pat . . . real lyrical. Know what I mean?

M. D. - Evan was more of a blues king. He could play you a blues like nobody else. Naturally Bunk was different. Bunk could play any kind of music. But as the blues go, I don't know of anybody around here who could beat Evan Thomas.

H. P. - Evan could come to those small towns, you know, and just decide he didn't have anything to do so he would sit in the window of the club or hall where he was playing and blow his trumpet and drink. And do you know, that night there would be a full house.

M. D. - At that time, that was called ballyhooing around here. They would put the band on the back of a flat-bed truck and drive around with the music blastin'. They wouldn't announce the dance . . . there was no television and very few people could afford a radio. If we were going to play, lets say in Franklin. O. K.? No advertisements . . . no nothing. We would go into town around five in the evening and head straight to the hall where we would set up our instruments on the back of a truck. When everything was ready the driver would take off with us playing our really hot numbers. He knew exactly where to go. He would bring us all over town. We would play a number here, play a number there, play a number here, and so on. Then the truck would end up back at the hall where we started. We would then set up our instruments and fool around until it was time for the dance to start. That night we would have a packed house.

H. P. - And people only knew about it since five o'clock.

M. D. - That was really something.

AUSTIN SONNIER - What kind of music did you play in these halls?

M. D. - Jazz. All of us played jazz. Jazz was the style of music people wanted to hear at that time.

H. P. - And the blues.

M. D. - And then there came a time when they switched from jazz to popular music.

H. P. - That's where the radio came in.

M. D. - Now it seems as if jazz is going to come back.

H. P. - When the radio became popular the bands began to have troubles. Because, if a man heard a song on the radio and he knew the name of it, he would come to the band and ask them to play it. If the musicians didn't know that song the first time they were asked to play it, it was alright. Now if they were playing there regular, when they went back they had to know that song. See, that's where the band had to spend money. And they were selling sheet music high in those days. You had to buy the whole arrangement. That was also where you separated the men from the little boys . . . You had to know how to read music.

II

M. D. - I started taking music lessons on the clarinet in New Iberia with Beauragard Adam's brother, Jimmy Adam. That's when I was going to school at the Howe Institute (the school in New Iberia where Jimmy Adam was the regular music teacher). It was a Baptist boarding school, and tuition was twelve dollars a month. That was a lot of money in those days, but my father could afford it. He raised cattle and hogs.

H. P. - Jimmy Adam was a powerful clarinet player . . . and a good teacher too. Him and my father-in-law, Gus Fontenette, could run any trumpet player crazy. The only one they couldn't get to was Bunk . . . and Evan.

M. D. - Those two fellows really could play together. So far as Gus, that man could make a trombone sing. I never heard a trombone player playing lead until I heard Gus. He could play his horn like it was a trumpet. Did it often too. He had a good lip.

H. P. - He had all kinds of mutes that he made himself to get certain sounds. He would even stick a kazoo in the trombone and get a sound that was out of this world. People really went crazy when they heard him play that thing.

I heard Bunk play the "Saint Louis Blues" with the Banner Band at your father's club in Parks one night. He and Gus and Jimmy shook the people up so much they had to play that tune almost all night. In those days, if the people liked a tune they wanted you to play it over and over. It wasn't like today . . . one time and that's it. You would take a three-minute break between tunes so that people could get back to their table or make a request. Then you would go into the next number.

M. D. - I remember Bunk Johnson when he was in New Orleans. That was a long time back . . . before Louis Armstrong left New Orleans.

H. P. - In 1929 after Evan's band broke up, he and Bunk were playing with the Banner Band. They played for a long time together. That two-trumpet style was something new, and the people really went for it. In 1932 Evan quit the Banner to start another group of his own. I was living in Crowley then, and he wanted me to join and play saxophone. I couldn't accept because I had gotten into a little trouble and had to leave town in a hurry. It was probably a good thing I did because ten days after I got home in New Iberia Evan was killed in Rayne. He had just organized his band. Bunk was there, Al Wilson was there, and I don't remember who else he had.

From what I heard, this fellow asked Evan to play "I'll Be Glad When You're Dead You Rascal You". The man really had it against Evan. And he had been to the pen and everything [He had served time in the state penitentiary.]. When he asked Evan to play that tune, Evan played it. Well, that was a custom in those days. If the band was asked for a number and they knew it, they would play it. So anyway, when they were just about to end the number, the man was coming on Evan with one of those Deer Hood knives. When Evan saw him he ran, tried to get out of his way. If the door would have opened to the outside instead of the inside, Evan might have gotten away from him. But he had to open the door and pull it back. I imagine when he pulled it back the fellow was right behind him and stabbed him. He still got out of the building though. He ran about a block and died on the steps of a church. Somebody mentioned something about the graveyard but that's not right. He died on the steps of a church. Evan was a good Catholic. He was raised Catholic.

A. S. - Why did this man kill him?

M. D. - The way I understand it, he had a relationship with the man's wife while he was in the penitentiary. Thats what it was all about.

H. P. - Yes. I can tell you a little more about that. His wife was a beautiful woman. I don't know if she didn't cause her father to get killed. She was one of those . . . moveable women.

A. S. - Do you remember this man's name?

M. D. - No. I don't remember his name but . . .

H. P. - John Gilbey was his name. He got killed in Rayne. He also killed a few people there too. He killed a police officer and got away. When he came back, they recognized him and that's when the shooting took place. He got a few of them before they were able to kill him though.

M. D. - I never did know his name. I wasn't here when that happened. Must have been in New Orleans or Baton Rouge.
  I played in the Tuxedo Band in New Orleans in 1927, and I knew Papa Celestin very well as a leader. He was a fine guy to deal with. He never did do too much playing then though. He played more during the end of his career than he ever did.

H. P. - I remember when he used to play in Cade all the time. He was a good friend to Bunk . . . all of the best musicians were. I knew Bunk from 1923 on up to the time of his death, and most of his good friends were people who knew a whole lot about music. As a man to talk to, he was the greatest. If it was about music or anything else, he was the type of man you enjoyed talking to. He was a drinking man . . . We all drink and we're all not the same person when we get drunk. We think we are but we're not. You got a different action when you drunk. Let me put it this way . . .

When Bunk was drinking, he was DRINKING. That's it. Just like me. When I'm drinking, I'm DRINKING.

M. D. - Look like Bunk enjoyed drinking. It was just one of those things. He was always a gentleman around women and that's what count.

H. P. - If he was drinking before a dance you might have to leave without him.

M. D. - He was sort of an independent fellow.

H. P. - He was independent.

M. D. - If he was supposed to be there at six and he couldn't make it, he just didn't care. He would continue to drink and have fun with his friends. He wasn't like the other fellows in the band who would break their necks trying to get there. No way. He's not gonna' do it.

III

M. D. - I came back here because I had to quit playing music. I didn't quit though. I would play occasionally. For instance, Harold would have a big job . . . they would come to see me, and I would leave with them. I was operating a nightclub with my other four brothers at the time, so I was able to leave anytime I wanted. I was just crazy about music. I never had a mind to stop playing unless I had to. See, the doctor wanted me to quit but I didn't intend to. He said my heart was not in the right condition to play music.

H. P. - Hypolite Charles studied music with my father. He was a lot younger, but they used to run together. And his father used to play in the same bands with him. He was a baritone horn player. August Charles. The baritone horns weren't like they are today. His was like a valve trombone.
 Tico also started young. Theophile Thibodeaux is his real name. He was a very good trumpet player. He had a brother that was called Tit Lut that was one of the best tail-gate trombone players around.

Théophile Thibodeaux was born in Parks, Louisiana, on December 16, 1890. He studied music with Peter Carey and played his first professional job in Carey's band "when he was so small he had to stand on a chair to be seen." He joined the United Brass Band in 1920 and stayed with them for twenty years. In 1940 he joined the Black Diamond Band. Members included: Simon Thibodeaux, his brother, trombone; George Thomas, guitar; John Gerrard, trumpet; Morris Dauphine, tenor saxophone; Alphonse Washington, trumpet; Buchanan Ledet, drums; Clay Derussell, bass; and Garland Stewart, vocals. He also played with the Washington Band from Cade, Louisiana, and with the Thibodeaux Band, a group he co-led with his brother, Simon, on trombone.

M. D. - They had a family orchestra.

H. P. - Because everybody was married to one another. The trombone player (Simon Thibodeaux) was married to my father's sister. Theophile and Simon got together with the Gerrard Band. That was another family affair from St. Martinville. They later organized the Black Diamond Band in Parks. John Gerrard was a fairly good trumpet player.

M. D. - He was with Clayborne Williams for a while.

H. P. - He also played with Guitar Slim. He wasn't much of a reader. Played mostly by ear.

M. D. - He couldn't read at all. That's what I heard. Could he?

H. P. - Yes he could. I seen him doing some reading. When we (the Banner Orchestra) went to Houston, Texas, at the St. Nicholas Hall in the

Third Ward, I met him and he was playing in the Mitchell Orchestra. That was one of the largest bands in Houston at that time. And it was a reading band.

M. D. - He was an ace player and shouldn't have wasted his time over here. If he would have gone to one of the big cities up North he could have been great. What happened to him was he married the band manager's daughter and just couldn't get away.

H. P. - Not to get off the subject . . . but. Did you know that Bunk played tuba around 1945 and '46? He played mostly tuba for a while. Not very many people know that. He didn't have any teeth in the front. He also worked at the rice mill, driving a truck. The man did not mind working.
    While I was in the army Russell [William] and Louis Armstrong took him to New Orleans to Dr. Duhe [Bechet] and had some teeth made for him.

M. D. - That was his excuse for not playing. He didn't have any teeth.

H. P. - Yeah. Well, they got him some. Hell, they knew they had something good. They even gave him a horn . . . Louis Armstrong did. I think Red Nicholas did the same thing. Bunk had a gold horn and a silver one too.

M. D.- At one time, if he decided to play with you, he had to borrow a horn.

H. P. - Do you know the picture of him in the suit, with the gold horn? That was my horn. He had to borrow it to take the picture. Still, he had lot of respect as a musician. Clarinet players like Lawrence Duhé and Jimmy Adam were always ready to play with him. Joe Oliver used to write to him all the time . . . .

M. D. - While I attended boarding school I took private clarinet lessons with Jimmy Adam. I would go to him after school and he would always have a half-gallon of moonshine around. He used to really like his booze. A heck of a clarinet player though.

H. P. - His father used to sell it. And you talk about a good musician. He taught all of his children to play music. He was a drummer. Mr. Adam could take drumsticks and play a roll that would sound like he was dropping BB's on the drum.

M. D. - I studied with Lorenzo Tio in New Orleans also. He used to love his juice too.

H. P. - All of them did.

M. D. - I don't ever remember Tio playing for blacks. They always played a kind of high-class music that whites liked.

I played a lot of funerals in New Orleans . . . and Baton Rouge too. Any musician that wanted to play in these parades could play. It was just like sittin'-in.

VII

THE BANNER ORCHESTRA

According to some of the more musically discerning, the Banner Orchestra of New Iberia was, by far, the best large ensemble in the area. Not only did it provide a wide array of current popular sounds, but it also hosted the best reading and improvising musicians from the New Iberia area. The orchestra included such stalwart jazzmen as George Lewis, Bunk Johnson, Lawrence Duhé, and Evan Thomas as well as a large number of lesser known but equally talented locals. And because of its high business and music standards along with its many years of existence it had a roster of more musicians than any other in the area.

Gustave Fontenette was twenty years old when he formed the Banner Orchestra. Its original membership consisted of, according to son-in-law Harold Potier, nine musicians: two reeds, two trumpets, trombone, banjo, piano, bass, and drums. Potier recalls that

> Gus was a good musician and was able to attract good musicians. My father was one of the original trumpet players with the band. And he was one of the few cornet or trumpet players who could compete sound-wise with Gus. You see, Gus was a real loud trombone player and my father also played hard and loud. In fact, they called him 'Iron Man' because of his power.
>
> Another trumpet with the original orchestra was Pops Hamilton (George Hamilton). He was from New Iberia. He lived there, not far from Gus's place, for a long time. Then he moved to New Orleans. And he played with a lot of famous people there.
>
> Gus started off with an orchestra. He had played with some other bands around town before he decided to start his own. He knew music and he believed in doing things right.

Gustave Fontenette was born in New Iberia on December 15, 1888, around the time jazz started to take form in New Orleans. He studied music as a child and was performing professionally by the time he reached his early teens. His father, who made a living as a barber, was also involved in music. And Gustave's aunt, Lila, was a professional piano player. She was married to trombonist Frankie Dusen. So music was obviously a strong element among Gustave's early influences.

Because of the difficulties involved in making a decent living in New Iberia solely on music, Gustave went into the trade of his father, barbering. He, in fact, spent most of his life as a barber, earning extra money as a bartender and bandleader. Music was his life though. It was his true profession and main interest. Cornetist Hypolite Charles, who was three years younger than Gustave, remembers his friend as "a serious business man and a real good musician who learned to master many other musical instruments beside the trombone".

By 1908 Gustave had settled down to married life and decided to form his own band. Because of his work as a professional musician with a number of area bands he had made quite a few important contacts, and his attempt to start a band came up against little friction. He had no trouble attracting musicians from throughout the area as well as from New Orleans.

During its years as a working unit the Banner Orchestra played just about every top nightclub in the New Iberia area. One of the advantages that black bands had over white bands in Louisiana during that time was that they were able to play for both black and white clubs and dances. And the Banner Orchestra was popular in both arenas. "Everybody wanted the Banner Orchestra," remininsces Potier,

> When the band was really hot you had to book the job almost a year in advance. And during Lent (when Catholic South Louisiana was literally closed to fun) we would travel all the way to Beaumont and Port Arthur, Texas, to play dances. In fact we once played opposite Count Basie in Beaumont. He was at one end of the hall and we were at the other end. We would each take a turn to play a number.

Like most bands anywhere, the Banner had its frequent personnel changes, perhaps a bit more frequent than any of the other aggregations in Southwest Louisiana. But the quality of musicianship was always high with each new player.

Pianist Mercedes Potier recalls:

> My father's orchestra had Bunk Johnson playing trumpet and tuba sometimes. He was world famous. Lawrence Duhé was world famous. Evan Thomas came from Crowley to play trumpet.

George Lewis came from New Orleans to play clarinet. Ed Redium, Walter Brundy, Glossey Roy, Jimmy Adam all played in the band at one time or another.

Although it had its ups and downs, the Banner Orchestra remained popular around Southwest Louisiana for almost forty years.

The following is a partial list of Banner Orchestra members:

Gustave Fontenette (Leader) - trombone
Robert Stafford - drums
Jimmy Adam - clarinet
Landers Roy - banjo
Edwin Redium - violin, banjo
Tom Avery - saxophones, bass
Hypolite Potier - cornet
Bunk Johnson - trumpet, tuba
Evan Thomas - trumpet
Beauragard Adam - violin, trumpet, alto saxophone
Janus Adam - drums
Roy Evan - drums
Morris Dauphine - clarinet, alto saxophone
Walter Brundy - drums
Son Adam - violin, guitar
Joe Banks - cornet
Abbie "Chinee" Foster - drums, vocals
Joe Gabriel - violin, mandolin
George "Pops" Hamilton - trumpet, bass
James Lewis - clarinet, saxophones
Lewis Landry - bass
Gabriel Ledet · bass
Wilfred Bocage - saxophones
Abraham Martin - banjo
Mary Ella Fontenette Oliver - piano
Mercedes Potier - piano
Harold Potier - trumpet
William Burner - piano
Allan Pratt - vocals
Chester Richardson - tenor saxophone, vocals
Glossey Roy - saxophones
John Saunders - bass, drums
Bob Thomas - trombone
Carlton Wilson - saxophones, bass

VIII

OTHER AREA BANDS AND MUSICIANS

Some of the more popular area bands and their personnel:

HYPOLITE CHARLES BAND (Parks)

Hypolite Charles . . . cornet (leader)
Theophile Thibodeaux . . . cornet
Hypolite Potier . . . cornet
Simon Thibodeaux . . . trombone
August Charles . . . baritone horn
Gabriel Ledet . . . bass
George W. Adam . . . drums

ADAM JENKINS BAND (New Iberia)

Janus Adam . . . drums
Son Adam . . . violin, guitar
Frank Brown . . . trumpet
Harold Potier . . . trumpet
Edwin Redium . . . violin, banjo

BLACK EAGLES BAND (Crowley)

Evan Thomas . . . trumpet (leader)
Lawrence Duhé . . . clarinet
Robert Goby . . . saxophone
Joseph "Kid" Avery . . . trombone
Abraham Martin . . . banjo
Walter Thomas . . . drums
Minor Decou . . . bass
Bunk Johnson . . . trumpet
George Lewis . . . clarinet
Beauragard Adam . . . violin, trumpet, alto saxophone

Brazlee Harrison . . . trombone
Frank Brown . . . trumpet
Sam Dutrey, Jr. . . . clarinet
Charles Hamilton . . . piano, banjo
George "Pop" Hamilton . . . trumpet, alto horn, bass, tuba
Baker Millian . . . tenor saxophone
Harold Potier . . . trumpet
Mercedes Potier . . . piano
Bob Thomas . . . trombone
Chester Zardis . . . bass

ADAM FAMILY BAND (New Iberia)

Jimmy Adam . . . clarinet
Beauragard Adam . . . trumpet, violin
Gertrude Adam . . . piano
Melba Adam . . . piano, vocals
Janus Adam . . . drums
George W. Adam . . . drums (leader)

WASHINGTON BAND (Cade)

Alfraze Washington . . . trumpet
Hamilton Washington . . . trombone, banjo
Carlton Wilson . . . saxophone, bass
Harold Potier . . . trumpet
Warnest Dequir . . . drums
Bernard Durea . . . vocals
Edwin Redium . . . violin, banjo
Theophile Thibodeaux . . . trumpet

VITALE BAND (Loreauville)

Jules Day . . . trumpet
Tom Vitale . . . trumpet
Louis Vitale . . . trombone

August Charles . . . baritone horn
George W. Adam . . . drums
Pierre Vitale . . . bass
Hypolite Charles . . . cornet

UNITED BRASS BAND (Parks)

Hypolite Potier . . . cornet
Hypolite Charles . . . cornet
Theophile Thibodeaux . . . trumpet
Simon Thibodeaux . . . trombone
Amerson Washington . . . trombone
August Charles . . . baritone horn
Buchanan Ledet . . . drums

YELPIN' HOUNDS (Crowley)

Jules Babin . . . trumpet, trombone
Harold Potier . . . trumpet
"Tenance" . . . c melody saxophone
Quintard Miller . . . violin
Son Adam . . . violin, guitar
Sonny Hebert . . . bass
Beauragard Adam . . . violin, trumpet, alto saxophone
Joseph "Kid" Avery . . . trombone
Baker Millian . . . tenor saxophone
Mercedes Potier . . . piano

BLACK DIAMOND BAND (Parks)

Theophile Thibodeaux . . . trumpet
Alfraze Washington . . . trumpet
Morris Dauphine . . . alto saxophone
Simon Thibodeaux . . . trombone
George Thomas . . . guitar
Clay Deroussell . . . bass

Buchanan Ledet . . . drums
Garland Steward . . . vocals
John Gerrard . . . trumpet

MARTEL FAMILY BAND (Opelousas)

Bert Martel . . . trumpet
Dayton Martel . . . trumpet, trombone
Hillery Martel . . . violin
Willie Martel . . . banjo
Joe Darensbourg . . . clarinet
Bradford Gordon . . . violin
various bass and drum players

DON FELTON BAND (Opelousas)

Don Felton . . . drums (leader)
Bert Martel . . . trumpet
Claxton Norman . . . trumpet
Bradford Gordon . . . violin
Mary Bernard . . . vocals
Charlotte Lemelle . . . piano
Miller Guidry
Lawrence Henderson

BUNK JOHNSON BAND (New Iberia)

Bunk Johnson . . . trumpet (leader)
Lewis Landry . . . bass
George "Pop" Hamilton . . . trumpet, tuba
Baker Millian . . . tenor saxophone
Mercedes Potier . . . piano
Gus Fontenette . . . trombone
Hypolite Potier . . . cornet
George Lewis . . . clarinet

Other area bands of note:

    BEAUREGARD ADAM BAND (Cade)
    FRANK BROWN BAND (Lafayette)
    THIBODEAUX BROTHERS BAND (Parks)
    JOHN DANIEL ORCHESTRA (Jeanerette)
    PALLET BROTHERS BAND (New Iberia)
    CUDDICK BAND (New Iberia)
    LIONS BRASS BAND (New Iberia)
    STEVE ADAM TRIO (Jeanerette)
    JOSEPH OGER BAND (Crowley)
    GERRARD FAMILY BAND (St. Martinville)
    VICTORY BAND (New Iberia)
    NIGHT HAWKS (New Iberia)
    BAT BROWN ORCHESTRA (Lafayette)

SOURCES

All interviews were conducted by the author.

Interviews with HAROLD POTIER (New Iberia) June 1973, August 1973, February 1974, December 1976, May 1978, May 1981.

Interviews with MERCEDES POTIER (New Iberia) August 1974, December 1976.

Interview with MORRIS DAUPHINE (New Iberia) May 1974.

Interview with BEAURAGARD ADAM (Cade) May 1974.

Interview with JOHN SANDERS (Jeanerette) January 1974.

Interview with CHESTER RICHARDSON (New Iberia) December 1973.

Interview with MAUDE BALQUE JOHNSON (New Orleans) November 1973.

Interviews with HYPOLITE CHARLES (Parks) June 1973, August 1973, January 1974, May 1977, March 1978.

Interviews with ROSE JEFFERSON CHARLES (Parks) August 1973, March 1978.

Interview with BERT MARTEL (Opelousas) June 1973.

Interview with BRADFORD GORDEN (Opelousas) June 1973.

Interview with THEOPHILE THIBODEAUX (Parks) August 1973.

Interview with LOUIS LANDRY (New Iberia) February 1974.

Interview with CHESTER ZARDIS (New Orleans) May 1982.

Interview with ROSY DUHÉ LEWIS (Lafayette) April 1986.

Interviews with WILLIAM DAUPHINE (Lafayette) March 1985, August 1985, January 1986.

Interview with ANTHONY BROWN (El Paso, Texas) July 1971.